THIS BOOK
WAS PRESENTED TO:

_____

FROM:

_____

ON THIS DAY:

_____

978-1-4336-4870-0

Published by B&H Publishing Group
Nashville, Tennessee

3 4 5 6 7 8 • 21 20 19 18 17

100 GALACTIC DEVOTIONS

DISCOVERING THE GOD OF THE UNIVERSE

by Abbey Land

B&H KIDS

Nashville, Tennessee

INTRODUCTION

My dad finished building my tree house right before my birthday. I spent hours in there. I would sweep the floor, play house, and sometimes I would even crawl up there at night to look at the stars. We lived in the country, and the view was beautiful. On a clear night, the stars filled the sky. When I looked at the sky, I knew only the God of the universe could have created such beauty.

How much do you know about the God of the universe? What questions do you have about this earth God created? Do you ever wonder exactly what God's plan is for you or how you are supposed to live? God designed this world with you in mind. Living life is all about your relationship with God. Did you know God wants to have a relationship with you?

This book is divided into five sections that follow Galactic Surveyors VBS. The first section focuses on the relationship God wants to have with you. You'll discover how this relationship began and how God designed the world. In the next section, you'll learn about how sin messes up the relationship. In the third section, you'll see how God had a plan to send Jesus to help with the sin problem. Section four is all about how Jesus died for you and why He did. The last section helps you learn more about how to continue your relationship with God. Some verses will come directly from the Bible story for each day, while others will help you learn more about the subject for each section.

After each devotion, you'll see a section labeled "Family Talk Time." These questions give you the chance to talk with your family about what you've just read. Some questions are fun, and other questions may take a little more time to think about before answering. Talking with your family will help you apply the lessons you've been learning to your life. Now, are you ready to take a closer look at what the God of the universe has planned for you?

DISCOVERING THE GOD OF THE UNIVERSE

The five sections are based on each day of Galactic Surveyors. This means that what is taught on day one of VBS is covered in the first section of this book. This gives you the opportunity to take a closer look at what you learned in VBS each day.

SECTION 1: THE RELATIONSHIP BEGAN

Bible Passage: Genesis 1:1–2, 26–31; John 1:1, 14

Bonus Verse: He is before all things, and by Him all things hold together.—Colossians 1:17

The Point: The God who created everything wants a relationship with us.

SECTION 2: THE RELATIONSHIP BROKEN

Bible Passage: Genesis 3
Bonus Verse: For all have sinned and fall short of the glory of God.—Romans 3:23
The Point: Sin messed everything up, but God is still in control.

SECTION 3: THE RESTORATION PROMISED

Bible Passage: Isaiah 7:14; Matthew 1:18–24; Luke 2:22–38
Bonus Verse: The Word became flesh and took up residence among us.—John 1:14
The Point: God sent His Son, Jesus, to be the Savior of the world.

SECTION 4: THE RELATIONSHIP RESTORED

Bible Passage: Mark 15:22–16:7
Bonus Verse: In Christ, God was reconciling the world to Himself, not counting their trespasses against them.
—2 Corinthians 5:19
The Point: Jesus gave His life to be my Savior.

SECTION 5: THE RELATIONSHIP CONTINUES

Bible Passage: John 21:1–19; Acts 1:4, 8
Bonus Verse: But the Counselor, the Holy Spirit–the Father will send Him in My name–will teach you all things and remind you of everything I have told you.—John 14:26
The Point: Even though I mess up, God still loves me and will never leave me.

1

OVER IT ALL

KEY VERSE: COLOSSIANS 1:15-16

He is the image of the invisible God, the firstborn over all creation. For everything was created by Him, in heaven and on earth, the visible and the invisible, whether thrones or dominions or rulers or authorities—all things have been created through Him and for Him.

God created everything and is over everything. The stars in the sky? He knows exactly how many are there. The temperature of the sun? God knows the exact degree, because He made the sun. God created everything you see and everything you can't see, too! Here's the best part. The God of the universe wants a relationship with you. God knows everything about you, and He has a plan for you. Are you ready to learn more about the God of the universe?

FAMILY TALK TIME

ASK YOUR KID:

What's a question you have about earth that you know God could answer for you?

ASK YOUR PARENT:

What's your favorite thing on earth that God created?

THE BEGINNING

KEY VERSE: GENESIS 1:1

In the beginning God created the heavens and the earth.

Think about the last picture you drew. You created it. You decided what colors to use and how it would look. Before you began drawing, the paper was blank. Before God created the heavens and earth, nothing existed. Both the earth and the heavens began when God created them. When God made the heavens and the earth, He was just getting started!

FAMILY TALK TIME

ASK YOUR KID:

Why is it important to know God created heaven and earth?

ASK YOUR PARENT:

When do you first remember hearing God created the heavens and the earth?

IN THE DARK

KEY VERSE: GENESIS 1:2

Now the earth was formless and empty, darkness covered the surface of the watery depths, and the Spirit of God was hovering over the surface of the waters.

Being in the complete dark with no light can be a little scary. When God created the earth, it was empty and dark. Why? Because God hadn't created light yet. God is the Creator of light. Isn't that incredible? Who was hovering over the water? The Spirit of God was hovering. God existed before anything else did. He created everything and has ultimate control over everything. Even in the dark, God was there and still is today.

FAMILY TALK TIME

ASK YOUR KID:

Have you ever been somewhere that was completely dark? How did it make you feel?

ASK YOUR PARENT:

Were you afraid of the dark when you were my age? How do you feel about being in the dark now?

4

RULER OF THE ANIMALS

KEY VERSE: GENESIS 1:26

Then God said, "Let Us make man in Our image, according to Our likeness. They will rule the fish of the sea, the birds of the sky, the livestock, all the earth, and the creatures that crawl on the earth."

Has one of your parents ever said, "You're in charge!" to you as he or she stepped out of the room for a moment? How does being in charge feel? God made man the ruler over everything on earth! All animals in the sky, on land, and in water are under the care of man. Who is ruling over everything God created? You are, and so are all of the other people in the world. Are you up for the challenge?

FAMILY TALK TIME

ASK YOUR KID:

How do you think God expects you
to rule over everything on earth?

ASK YOUR PARENT:

Why do you think God put man in charge
of everything on earth?

IN HIS IMAGE

KEY VERSE: GENESIS 1:27

So God created man in His own image; He created him in the image of God; He created them male and female.

When you look in a mirror, what do you see? You see an image of you, a reflection of yourself. God created man in His image. This means God created people to be like Him. He also chose to make people male and female. God made you, and He made you to be like Him. When others look at you, God wants them to see Him in you.

FAMILY TALK TIME

ASK YOUR KID:

How do you think others would describe you?

ASK YOUR PARENT:

Why is it important for you to remember that you were created in God's image?

FILL THE EARTH

KEY VERSE: GENESIS 1:28

God blessed them, and God said to them,
"Be fruitful, multiply, fill the earth, and subdue it.
Rule the fish of the sea, the birds of the sky,
and every creature that crawls on the earth."

What happens when you multiply two numbers together?
You get a bigger number! God created the earth and wants
it to be filled with people. He wants people to marry and
have children, grandchildren, and great-grandchildren.
When a baby is born, God rejoices! God wants His people to
take care of the earth along with all the animals living on it.

FAMILY TALK TIME

ASK YOUR KID:

What's the craziest looking creature
you've ever seen?

ASK YOUR PARENT:

How are people supposed to rule over
the animals God created?

7

PLANTING SEED

KEY VERSE: GENESIS 1:29

God also said, "Look, I have given you every seed-bearing plant on the surface of the entire earth and every tree whose fruit contains seed. This food will be for you."

God created the heavens and the earth, man and woman, and animals. He made sure to provide food for all the living creatures too! He didn't just give them food ready to eat; God created seeds so they could grow food and always have the food they need. Fruits, vegetables, and many other plants continue to reproduce because of seeds. God thought of every detail to care for people on earth.

FAMILY TALK TIME

ASK YOUR KID:

What's your favorite food to eat that has seeds?

ASK YOUR PARENT:

What plants have you watched grow from a seed?

EAT YOUR GREENS

KEY VERSE: GENESIS 1:30

"For all the wildlife of the earth, for every bird of the sky, and for every creature that crawls on the earth—everything having the breath of life in it. I have given every green plant for food." And it was so.

How many creatures live on earth? Take a moment and make a list. You probably had to stop short because there are so many animals! All the animals you listed, plus many more, have the "breath of life" in them. God promised to give creatures all the green plants for food. Not only did God have a plan to care for people, He created ways to continue to provide food for all the animals roaming the earth. This God who created all this wants a relationship with you.

FAMILY TALK TIME

ASK YOUR KID:

What animals have you seen eating plants?

ASK YOUR PARENT:

Why do you think God found it important
to provide food for animals?

IT'S ALL GOOD

KEY VERSE: GENESIS 1:31

God saw all that He had made, and it was very good.
Evening came and then morning: the sixth day.

What happens if you are following a recipe and you leave out an ingredient? It probably won't turn out very good. When God made the world and everything in it, He didn't make a single mistake. Every single thing He made was good and free of sin. As a human in a sinful world, you'll always make mistakes, and that's okay. Just remember the God who is in charge of everything has never made a mistake.

FAMILY TALK TIME

ASK YOUR KID:

What's one of your favorite things
God has made?

ASK YOUR PARENT:

When do you have to remind yourself that
everything God made was good?

10

THE WORD

KEY VERSE: JOHN 1:1

In the beginning was the Word, and the Word was with God, and the Word was God.

I was in a choir at church that sang the words to John 1:1 in an anthem. When the choir sang the song, different parts of the choir sang the words to this verse at different times. Those listening to the singing couldn't tell when the verse started or ended for each part because it all flowed together. It was a beautiful blending of voices that showed how the Word has no beginning and no end but continues forever! The Word of God always has been, it is, and it always will be.

FAMILY TALK TIME

ASK YOUR KID:

What's one of your favorite verses from God's Word?

ASK YOUR PARENT:

When you have trouble understanding the meaning of a verse, how do you figure it out?

11

IN THE FLESH

KEY VERSE: JOHN 1:14

The Word became flesh and took up residence among us.
We observed His glory, the glory as the One and
Only Son from the Father, full of grace and truth.

How does word become flesh? Flesh is skin, right? While this verse may be confusing at first, the next sentence makes it clear the "flesh" is Jesus! When God created the world and everything in it, He had the ultimate plan in mind. Jesus is a part of that plan, and so are you. When Jesus walked on earth, He fulfilled a promise from long ago. Not only did Jesus come to earth, He came "full of grace and truth."

FAMILY TALK TIME

ASK YOUR KID:

What's one reason you are glad
Jesus came to earth?

ASK YOUR PARENT:

Why is it good Jesus is described
as "full of grace"?

12

HOLDING IT TOGETHER

KEY VERSE: COLOSSIANS 1:17

*He is before all things, and by Him
all things hold together.*

Who makes sure you have food to eat? Who drives you
where you need to go? You depend on your parents a lot to
take care of you until you grow up. The great news is you
can depend on God forever. He is in control of everything
and knows everything from how many grains of sand are
on the beach to how many stars are in the sky. Aren't you
glad God is in charge and cares for you?

FAMILY TALK TIME

ASK YOUR KID:

What is one thing you worry about?

ASK YOUR PARENT:

What is one thing you are glad to know God takes care of in your life?

FOR HIM

KEY VERSE: 1 CORINTHIANS 8:6

For us there is one God, the Father. All things are from Him, and we exist for Him. And there is one Lord, Jesus Christ. All things are through Him, and we exist through Him.

You don't ever have to wonder, *Why am I here?* God created you to worship Him and tell others about Him. You wouldn't exist without God. You were created for a purpose. You are here because God wanted you here, and He controls all things. How will you find out God's plan for you? One way is what you are doing right now, reading and studying God's Word.

FAMILY TALK TIME

ASK YOUR KID:

How are you going to learn more about God's plan for you?

ASK YOUR PARENT:

What is something that has happened in your life that you know was from God?

14

NO IMITATIONS

KEY VERSE: DEUTERONOMY 4:35

You were shown these things so that you would know that the Lord is God; there is no other besides Him.

What's your favorite fruit-flavored, slushed-ice drink? Do you enjoy watermelon, banana, strawberry, or grape? While the drink may taste similar to the fruit, the truth is it isn't the real thing. But you don't have to wonder if God is the real deal. No other god exists except God the Father, the Son, and the Holy Spirit. He is above all things and in all things, and He wants a relationship with you.

FAMILY TALK TIME

ASK YOUR KID:

How do people compare to God?

ASK YOUR PARENT:

Why would anyone want to say
they are like God?

NEVER ALONE

KEY VERSE: DEUTERONOMY 31:6

Be strong and courageous; don't be terrified or afraid of them. For it is the L<small>ORD</small> your God who goes with you; He will not leave you or forsake you.

Getting separated from a group or your parent in a busy place can be scary. Suddenly you are all alone, and you aren't sure what to do. With God, you are never alone. God doesn't break promises, and He promises never to leave you. When find yourself afraid or worried, remember that God is with you wherever you go. You can trust in God to be with you.

FAMILY TALK TIME

ASK YOUR KID:

How do you normally act
when you are afraid?

ASK YOUR PARENT:

When was a time you were afraid?
What did you do?

16

ALWAYS THERE

KEY VERSE: DEUTERONOMY 31:8

The LORD is the One who will go before you.
He will be with you; He will not leave you
or forsake you. Do not be afraid or discouraged.

Have you ever seen a shooting star? You have to look up at the sky at just the right moment to experience the wonder. You don't have to look at just the right moment to catch God. God was before you, is with you now, and always will be. Knowing God is always there is not a sometimes, random happening like witnessing a shooting star is. God's presence is a guaranteed part of life.

FAMILY TALK TIME

ASK YOUR KID:

What is something amazing
you've seen in the sky?

ASK YOUR PARENT:

When have you seen something in
the sky that has encouraged you?

17

NO SATELLITE NEEDED

KEY VERSE: JOSHUA 1:9

"Haven't I commanded you; be strong and courageous? Do not be afraid or discouraged, for the Lord your God is with you wherever you go."

Satellites orbit in outer space for many reasons. They help with communication in many different ways. One way is with cell phone service. Did you know cell phones can track your every move, even recognize popular places? God doesn't need a tracking device to know where you are. He promises to be with you no matter where you go. Anytime you need God, you can call out to Him, and He will be there for you.

FAMILY TALK TIME

ASK YOUR KID:

Where have you been that you've felt God was with you?

ASK YOUR PARENT:

Why is it important that you know where I am and what I'm doing?

18

COMMANDED BY GOD

KEY VERSE: HEBREWS 11:3

By faith we understand that the universe was created by God's command, so that what is seen has been made from things that are not visible.

Optical illusions are fun to study. One minute you think you see one thing, and the next you've discovered a completely different image! Look outside for a moment. What do you notice? All of nature that you see is made by God. Clouds? God made them. The sun or stars shining brightly? God made that happen too. Everything you see began with God's commands. When you recognize God's power and abilities, you get to know Him more quickly.

FAMILY TALK TIME

ASK YOUR KID:

What's the most amazing thing
you've ever seen in nature?

ASK YOUR PARENT:

Why is it important to help others recognize
God's power over heaven and earth?

19

DESERVING OF PRAISE

KEY VERSE: REVELATION 4:11

Our Lord and God, You are worthy to receive glory and honor and power, because You have created all things, and because of Your will they exist and were created.

Why do you cheer for a sports team? Perhaps your team made a great play, a fabulous comeback, or a good move, and you want to celebrate and congratulate the team. Why does God deserve glory and honor from you? God rules over everything. The beautiful night sky with a full moon? God created the moon, stars, and sky. He deserves praise, honor, and glory above anyone or anything else on the planet.

FAMILY TALK TIME

ASK YOUR KID:

What is your favorite way to show God praise?

ASK YOUR PARENT:

How do you give God glory for something
that has happened in your life?

GOD ABOVE ALL ELSE

KEY VERSE: NEHEMIAH 9:6

*You alone are Yahweh. You created the heavens,
the highest heavens with all their host, the earth
and all that is on it, the seas and all that is in them. You give
life to all of them. and the heavenly host worships You.*

When a room receives a makeover on a television show, often you'll see the designer get the credit for making the room look amazing. Guess who gets the credit for all of creation? God does. Guess who deserves praise for everything? God does. Guess who wants to be a part of your daily life and help you make decisions about everything in your life? God does.

FAMILY TALK TIME

ASK YOUR KID:

How can God be a part of your daily life?

ASK YOUR PARENT:

How is God a part of your daily life?

DON'T TOUCH

KEY VERSE: GENESIS 3:2-3

The woman said to the serpent, "We may eat the fruit from the trees in the garden. But about the fruit of the tree in the middle of the garden, God said, 'You must not eat it or touch it, or you will die.'"

Have you ever been told not to touch something? How difficult is it to follow that rule? Eve is the woman in Genesis 3:2–3. God specifically told her not to eat or touch the fruit of a specific tree. Do you think this was a hard direction to follow? Following directions isn't always easy, but knowing God's commandments is easy. God wants you to listen and follow His commands.

FAMILY TALK TIME

ASK YOUR KID:

What's the hardest command you've ever had to follow?

ASK YOUR PARENT:

Why is it important to follow God's command?

THE BEST HIDING PLACE

KEY VERSE: GENESIS 3:8

Then the man and his wife heard the sound of the Lord God walking in the garden at the time of the evening breeze, and they hid themselves from the Lord God among the trees of the garden.

One time when I was a kid, I was with a lot of family and needed a break. I found the perfect hiding place in a quiet room behind a piece of furniture. People would walk by and had no idea I was in there! I could hear what was happening all around me, but I was able to be alone too. It was the best hiding place!

Adam and Even knew they'd made a mistake. They'd done the one thing God had told them not to do, so they were hiding from Him. Is that even possible? No, God knows exactly where you are at all times. God will always be with you. Let this be a comfort to you.

FAMILY TALK TIME

ASK YOUR KID:

Why is it good to know that God always knows where you are?

ASK YOUR PARENT:

Where was your best hiding place as a kid?

23

WHERE ARE YOU?

KEY VERSE: GENESIS 3:9

The LORD God called out to the man and said to him, "Where are you?"

Adam and Eve knew they had committed a sin by eating the fruit from the tree God said to stay away from. They chose to hide from God, and now God was asking Adam where He was. Why did God ask a question He already knew the answer to? God was offering Adam the chance to explain why he was hiding. God wanted Adam to admit that he had done wrong by not following God's command.

Does God know every single time you sin? Yes. Will God forgive you every time you sin? Absolutely. He forgives us when we ask Him to with a sincere apology.

FAMILY TALK TIME

ASK YOUR KID:

Have you ever hidden after you did something wrong so you wouldn't get in trouble?

ASK YOUR PARENT:

How hard is it to admit when you've made a mistake?

THE BLAME GAME

KEY VERSE: GENESIS 3:11-12

[God] asked, "Who told you that you were naked? Did you eat from the tree that I commanded you not to eat from?" Then the man replied, "The woman You gave to be with me—she gave me some fruit from the tree, and I ate."

Are you guilty of ever saying, "She made me do it," when you did something wrong? Adam knew what he had done was wrong, but he didn't want to take all the blame himself, so he chose to tell God how he got the fruit in the first place.

Adam made the choice to sin. When a person chooses to sin, no one else is to blame but that person. Eve gave Adam the fruit, but she didn't force him to eat it. He made the choice. What choice are you making? Are you blaming someone else when you sin, or are you choosing to be honest with God and admit when you do wrong?

FAMILY TALK TIME

ASK YOUR KID:

Why might you try to blame someone else for something you've done wrong?

ASK YOUR PARENT:

Why is it better to admit when you are wrong instead of blaming someone else?

DON'T BE DECEIVED

KEY VERSE: GENESIS 3:13

The LORD God asked the woman, "What is this you have done?" And the woman said, "It was the serpent. He deceived me, and I ate."

Remember how Adam blamed Eve for eating the fruit? When God asked Eve about her choice, she quickly blamed the serpent. She told God that the serpent had tricked her into eating the fruit. The serpent was dishonest about the fruit, but Eve still made the choice to eat it.

It can be difficult to be caught doing wrong. You may be sad, ashamed, or mad that you made a poor choice, but you made it. God already knows every single sin you will commit; He loves you anyway. Instead of explaining how you were tricked into doing something, ask God for help not to commit the same sin again.

FAMILY TALK TIME

ASK YOUR KID:

Why do you think Eve told God the serpent tricked her?

ASK YOUR PARENT:

How do you keep from being tricked by people?

26

CONSEQUENCES

KEY VERSE: GENESIS 3:16

[God] said to the woman: I will intensify your labor pains; you will bear children in anguish.

For every action, there is a reaction. Has anyone ever told you that before? Sin has consequences. In this verse, God reveals one consequence for disobeying His command to not eat the fruit. He explains that Eve, and every woman after Eve, will experience pain during childbirth. God makes it clear that this is because Eve disobeyed.

Sin messes things up. You could blame Eve for all women who have pain when they have babies, but the truth is every single person on the planet sins. Consequences of sin are felt everywhere every day. God makes it very clear that although people mess up, He's still in control of everything.

FAMILY TALK TIME

ASK YOUR KID:

What's a consequence you've experienced
because of a sin you committed?

ASK YOUR PARENT:

How do the consequences of sin affect
the choices you make today?

THE PAIN OF DISOBEDIENCE

KEY VERSE: GENESIS 3:17

[God] said to Adam, "Because you listened to your wife's voice and ate from the tree about which I commanded you, 'Do not eat from it': The ground is cursed because of you. You will eat from it by means of painful labor all the days of your life."

Do you wonder what life was like for Adam and Eve before they sinned? I do! I think it must have been amazingly perfect. God made it clear that He would still provide food to eat, but it would come at a price. God promised painful labor for Adam like He did for Eve, but this time He was talking about working the ground. God explained this consequence wasn't short-term; it would last forever because sin had entered the world. Every sin has a consequence, and Adam's choice to make the first sin not only affected the ground but also made all people naturally sinful instead of good, the way God intended.

FAMILY TALK TIME

ASK YOUR KID:

How do you feel about the length of punishments you've received in the past? Did you think they were fair, too much, or too little?

ASK YOUR PARENT:

How do you decide how long a consequence should last when I make bad choices?

28

SAYING GOOD-BYE

KEY VERSE: GENESIS 3:23

The LORD God sent him away from the garden of Eden to work the ground from which he was taken.

Adam and Eve lived in the Garden of Eden, and it was all they had known as their home. After eating the forbidden fruit, God sent them away from it. This was another consequence of sin. How do you think Adam and Eve felt about leaving their home where they had always lived? Surely Adam and Eve were beginning to recognize they were going to remember and learn from their sin for the rest of their days. But God was still with Adam and Eve even though He sent them out of the garden. No matter how many times you mess up, God is still there for you. He is in control, and God wants you to talk to Him about everything happening in your life.

FAMILY TALK TIME

ASK YOUR KID:

What's the hardest good-bye
you've ever had to say?

ASK YOUR PARENT:

What's the longest move you've
ever had to make?

FALLING SHORT

KEY VERSE: ROMANS 3:23

For all have sinned and fall short of the glory of God.

I remember falling short of making a superior rating in a contest when I was younger. The room I was competing in was hot, there was a baby crying, and I didn't feel well. At the end of the competition, I received my first—and only—excellent rating instead of superior out of all my years of competition. I was disappointed in myself.

Everyone messes up. Everyone experiences disappointments. Everyone gets hurt feelings once in a while. Jesus is the only person to ever walk the earth and never commit a sin. The good news is God already knows you will sin, and He will be there to offer forgiveness every time you do.

FAMILY TALK TIME

ASK YOUR KID:

Why is it important to know
that everyone sins?

ASK YOUR PARENT:

How do you deal with disappointment
in yourself?

30

NOT EVEN ONE

KEY VERSE: ECCLESIASTES 7:20

There is certainly not a righteous man on the earth who does good and never sins.

The Milky Way is a galaxy of stars. While God knows the exact number of stars found in the Milky Way, scientists estimate it to contain about one hundred billion stars. If each star represented one person who has lived or is living on earth, not one single star would represent a sinless person. Can you believe it? No one can boast or brag about being the best person ever because that title belongs only to Jesus Christ, who lived on earth for a few decades. When you look up at the stars, remember to be thankful that God controls it all.

FAMILY TALK TIME

ASK YOUR KID:

Why can no one always be a good person?

ASK YOUR PARENT:

What's the difference between a good person and a sinless person?

31

GOOD, BETTER, BEST

KEY VERSE: ROMANS 3:9

What then? Are we any better? Not at all!
For we have previously charged that both
Jews and Gentiles are all under sin.

Multiple-choice tests can be tricky. One answer may be good, another may be better, but then there is the best answer. You have to read carefully to figure out which answer to choose. You don't have to worry about being in the good, better, or best category with God. God knows all people sin, and no one person is better than the next. Even better, God loves you no matter what sin you've committed. God only wants the best for you, and He will always be there when you ask for help.

FAMILY TALK TIME

ASK YOUR KID:

What's the best memory you have
of our family together?

ASK YOUR PARENT:

How does it feel to know God
loves everyone the same?

DON'T BE THE JUDGE

KEY VERSE: PSALM 143:2

Do not bring Your servant into judgment,
for no one alive is righteous in Your sight.

Why does she act that way? Didn't her mom teach her not to say those words? Have you ever had a thought like that before? Judging other's actions, behavior, and words might come easy to you, but the Bible is clear about passing judgment. God is specific in this verse that we are not to judge others. Guess who's job that is? God is ultimately in control over everything. Don't worry about what someone else is doing—or not doing; focus on living your life in a way that is pleasing to God.

FAMILY TALK TIME

ASK YOUR KID:

What's the difference between judging others and a judge who rules over a courtroom?

ASK YOUR PARENT:

How do you keep yourself from judging others?

THE ENTIRE WORLD

KEY VERSE: ROMANS 3:19

Now we know that whatever the law says speaks to those who are subject to the law, so that every mouth may be shut and the whole world may become subject to God's judgment.

What would happen if you told everyone in the world to freeze so you could count how many people are on earth? It would be impossible for billions of people to stand still that long! While a lot of people live in the world, God doesn't have to count them. Every single person in the whole wide world matters to God, and each person must answer to God for his or her actions. Remember, God is the judge of others. You are only responsible for what you say and do.

FAMILY TALK TIME

ASK YOUR KID:

How many people do you think
live on earth right now?

ASK YOUR PARENT:

Why do you think God is the ultimate
judge instead of people?

WORK IT OFF

KEY VERSE: ROMANS 3:20

For no one will be justified in His sight by the works of the law, because the knowledge of sin comes through the law.

Frequent customer cards are popular at different restaurants. Usually, the more you spend, the sooner you have worked your way into a free dessert or a discount on your next meal. When you receive the reward, you start all over again, earning points for the next time. Being a Christian doesn't work the same way. You cannot simply work your way into becoming a good Christian; first you need to study. The more you study your Bible, listen to your leaders, and ask questions, the more you will understand about how God wants you to live your life.

FAMILY TALK TIME

ASK YOUR KID:

What places have you earned special gifts
for being a good customer?

ASK YOUR PARENT:

What is one thing you do to learn
more about God's laws?

 35

ON REPEAT

KEY VERSE: ROMANS 5:12

Therefore, just as sin entered the world through one man, and death through sin, in this way death spread to all men, because all sinned.

The word *all* is a pronoun representing an amount. In today's verse, it means every single person. Does this message sound familiar? It should because it's repeated several times in the Bible. Why would God include the same words several times? Did He make a mistake? God never makes mistakes. Understanding that all people sin is an important part of becoming a Christian. No one on earth other than Jesus is perfect.

FAMILY TALK TIME

ASK YOUR KID:

What's something I have to tell
you over and over?

ASK YOUR PARENT:

Why do you think the Bible talks about all
people sinning in several verses?

WITHOUT SIN

KEY VERSE: 1 JOHN 1:8

If we say, "We have no sin," we are deceiving ourselves, and the truth is not in us.

Optical illusions may allow you to see one image one minute and another the next. It might even feel like your mind is playing tricks on you as you recognize different images are hidden within the same picture. You may have even wiggled your pencil back and forth to make it look like it was bending. This verse is a warning; if you begin to think you aren't guilty of sin, you are only lying to yourself. God is serious about sin, and He wants you to be ready to recognize it too.

FAMILY TALK TIME

ASK YOUR KID:

What optical illusions have you seen?

ASK YOUR PARENT:

What does it mean to deceive somebody?

DON'T FALL DOWN!

KEY VERSE: JAMES 3:2

We all stumble in many ways.

Does God care when you fall down? Of course He does! That's not what this verse is talking about, though. The "we" in this verse means everyone, and the word *stumble* refers to making mistakes. God knows you will mess up, and that's where Jesus comes in. Your friends, your leaders, your brothers or sisters, and even the pastor of your church all sin! What's the best thing to do when you fall down on the sidewalk? Get up, dust yourself off, and keep walking, right? Think of that the next time you sin. You don't have to stay stuck in wrongdoing. God wants you to get up and try again!

FAMILY TALK TIME

ASK YOUR KID:

What's the worst fall you've ever taken?

ASK YOUR PARENT:

What's your advice for moving on after making a big mistake?

38

DO GOOD

KEY VERSE: JAMES 4:17

*It is a sin for the person who knows to do
what is good and doesn't do it.*

How many choices do you make in a day? You decide when
you are going to wake up and get out of bed, you decide
whether or not to brush your teeth, and you choose what
you will eat for breakfast. That's just three of the things you
do in a day. You make the choice whether or not you will do
good each day. No one makes you decide; it is your decision. When you know you have the opportunity to do good
but you choose not to do so, it's a sin. Pray and ask God to
open your eyes to opportunities to do good.

FAMILY TALK TIME

ASK YOUR KID:

Why should you do good even if no one is around to notice?

ASK YOUR PARENT:

When have you chosen to do good when no one was looking?

ONE MAN MAKES THE DIFFERENCE

KEY VERSE: ROMANS 5:19

Just as through one man's disobedience the many were made sinners, so also through the one man's obedience the many will be made righteous.

Sometimes a game comes down to one player's performance. Will she be able to make the penalty shot? Will he get a base hit that brings a runner on third home? Will she catch the baton in the handoff and win the race? One player can make the difference between winning and losing a game. One man in the Bible chose sin, but one Man also changed the lives of everyone by choosing to sacrifice Himself for sins He never committed. Jesus made it possible to experience eternal life!

FAMILY TALK TIME

ASK YOUR KID:

Have others ever depended
on you to win a game?

ASK YOUR PARENT:

Why can one person's performance be so
important in a game being played as a team?

GRACE MULTIPLIED

KEY VERSE: ROMANS 5:20

The law came along to multiply the trespass. But where sin multiplied, grace multiplied even more.

One ant can find the single piece of popsicle that fell on the concrete. Before you know it, the ants have multiplied from one to thirty ants trying to get a taste of the sweet sugar. The bad news is sin can happen that way too. One lie can turn into two and then spiral way out of control. The good news is grace can multiply too! God offers forgiveness, over and over, that is far greater than any sin you commit.

FAMILY TALK TIME

ASK YOUR KID:

How many times do you think
God multiplies grace?

ASK YOUR PARENT:

What's the best explanation of
multiplication you've ever heard?

41

LOOK FOR THE SIGN!

KEY VERSE: ISAIAH 7:14

The Lord Himself will give you a sign: The virgin will conceive and have a son, and name him Immanuel.

Do you pay attention to road signs? If drivers didn't read signs and obey them, roads would be a big mess and dangerous! This verse is talking about a different kind of sign, though. Many years before Jesus was born, Isaiah shared the great news that Immanuel would be coming. Immanuel means Jesus! Can you imagine hearing such wonderful news?

FAMILY TALK TIME

ASK YOUR KID:

What's your favorite road sign
you've ever seen?

ASK YOUR PARENT:

Why do you think the Bible tells of Jesus'
coming so many years before His birth?

NO ORDINARY BIRTH ANNOUNCEMENT

KEY VERSE: MATTHEW 1:18

The birth of Jesus Christ came about this way: After His mother Mary had been engaged to Joseph, it was discovered before they came together she was pregnant by the Holy Spirit.

Mary and Joseph were engaged to be married. Before they were married, Mary discovered she was going to have a baby whose father wasn't Joseph. How do you think Joseph felt about this? How do you think Mary felt about this? Clearly, this wasn't going to be a normal birth. I imagine people didn't believe Mary when she explained what was happening. This baby wasn't going to be ordinary; the plan for this baby was much more extraordinary than for any other baby ever born.

FAMILY TALK TIME

ASK YOUR KID:

What do you think people said about Mary when they heard about her baby?

ASK YOUR PARENT:

How would you respond if Mary explained her pregnancy to you?

43

JOSEPH'S KINDNESS

KEY VERSE: MATTHEW 1:19

Her husband Joseph, being a righteous man, and not wanting to disgrace her publicly, decided to divorce her secretly.

Rather than embarrass Mary, Joseph decided he would handle the situation quietly. He couldn't be engaged to marry a woman who was pregnant with someone else's baby! But Joseph still cared about Mary and didn't want to make a big deal out of what had happened. Joseph made the choice to walk away from Mary. He didn't know it at the time, but God had much bigger plans for Joseph than he could ever imagine!

FAMILY TALK TIME

ASK YOUR KID:

How do you think Joseph felt about deciding to divorce Mary?

ASK YOUR PARENT:

How do you think Joseph made his decision to divorce Mary?

AM I DREAMING?

KEY VERSE: MATTHEW 1:20

After he had considered these things, an angel of the Lord suddenly appeared in him in a dream, saying, "Joseph, son of David, don't be afraid to take Mary as your wife, because what has been conceived in her is by the Holy Spirit."

God uses dreams throughout the Bible to teach someone a lesson or to tell someone what He wants them to do. Joseph's dream is responsible for changing his plan for how to deal with Mary. While he was planning to leave Mary, the angel told him not to be afraid. The angel echoed the same words Mary told him about her pregnancy. The Holy Spirit was responsible for Mary's pregnancy. While Joseph might not have understood why things were happening the way they were with Mary, he was willing to trust the news the angel delivered in his dream.

FAMILY TALK TIME

ASK YOUR KID:

What's the craziest dream you've ever had?

ASK YOUR PARENT:

Have you ever followed a plan or directions you didn't understand? How did things turn out?

45

THE SAVER OF SINS

KEY VERSE: MATTHEW 1:21

She will give birth to a son, and you are to name Him Jesus, because He will save His people from their sins.

Finally, you can see the big plan being put into action! First, God created the world and everything in it. Then sin entered the world with Adam and Eve's choice, and people had to face the consequences of sin. Then the angel told Joseph that the promised one is here. Not only was Jesus about to be born, but He was also going to save people from their sins. While this was revealed in a dream, it was about to quickly become reality. God's plan was beginning to unfold!

FAMILY TALK TIME

ASK YOUR KID:

How excited do you think Joseph was to hear what Jesus was coming to do?

ASK YOUR PARENT:

How do you think Joseph handled finding out he would be the earthly father of Jesus, the Son of God?

46

THE PROPHETS CALLED IT

KEY VERSE: MATTHEW 1:22-23

All this took place to fulfill what was spoken by the Lord through the prophet: See, the virgin will become pregnant and give birth to a son, and they will name Him Immanuel, which is translated "God is with us."

Does this verse sound a little familiar to you? Take a quick look at Isaiah 7:14 or turn back to devotion 41. What do you notice? It's the words from Isaiah 7:14 repeated right here in Matthew. One verse is in the Old Testament, and one is in the New Testament. The interesting thing is the book of Isaiah was written about seven hundred years before the book of Matthew! The prophets predicted Jesus would be born, and here it was really happening!

FAMILY TALK TIME

ASK YOUR KID:

What's the earliest memory you have?

ASK YOUR PARENT:

Have you ever predicted something would happen and it did?

NO QUESTIONS ASKED

KEY VERSE: MATTHEW 1:24

When Joseph got up from sleeping, he did as the Lord's angel had commanded him. He married her.

When someone gives you directions, do you do exactly what you are told the first time? Do you ask questions, or do you immediately go and do what you've been told? Joseph heard what the angel of the Lord said in his dream, and he when he woke up, he immediately obeyed. Joseph didn't ask why or how, or ask for time to think about what he wanted to do. The next time God asks you to do something, remember Joseph's example and follow it.

FAMILY TALK TIME

ASK YOUR KID:

How easy is it for you to follow directions without asking questions or giving excuses?

ASK YOUR PARENT:

What's the funniest excuse you've ever heard for not following directions?

48

BABY DEDICATION

KEY VERSE: LUKE 2:21-22

He was named Jesus—the name given by the angel before He was conceived. And when the days of their purification according to the law of Moses were finished, they brought Him up to Jerusalem to present Him to the Lord.

In many churches, parents have a special ceremony to dedicate their baby to the Lord. Proud parents and sometimes siblings stand in front of the congregation while the pastor prays over the child and dedicates him or her to the Lord. It's a special time for parents and the church to pray for the baby and promise to help raise the child in a way that pleases God. Mary and Joseph brought Jesus to be dedicated to God. As the promised Savior over the entire world, Jesus set the example for others to follow even as a baby.

FAMILY TALK TIME

ASK YOUR KID:

Why is it important to dedicate children to God?

ASK YOUR PARENT:

Was I dedicated as a child?

49

FRONT-ROW ACCESS

KEY VERSE: JOHN 1:14

The Word became flesh and took up residence among us. We observed His glory, the glory as the One and Only Son from the Father, full of grace and truth.

When an important government official comes to town, all the roads are closed, barriers are put up, and people line up to get a glimpse of the important person. These measures are put in place to protect the official from harm. That's not how Jesus wanted to be treated when He came to earth. He came to live among people, to teach, to heal, and to guide others in truth. You have front-row access to Jesus every single day.

FAMILY TALK TIME

ASK YOUR KID:

Why wasn't Jesus treated like a king
when He was on earth?

ASK YOUR PARENT:

Who is the most famous person
you've ever met?

50

IT'S NOT WHAT YOU THINK

KEY VERSE: JOHN 3:17

"For God did not send His Son into the world that He might condemn the world, but that the world might be saved through Him."

I just can't do anything right! That's what I thought one day when everything seemed to be going wrong. Some people think Jesus came to point out all the wrong things they are doing in life. While Jesus does know when you sin, He didn't come to earth to make a list of all the things you do wrong. Jesus came so He could save the world from sin! Instead of thinking about all the wrong things you've done, focus on doing the right things for God.

FAMILY TALK TIME

ASK YOUR KID:

What's the best choice you've made this week?

ASK YOUR PARENT:

What happens if you focus on the bad instead of the good?

51

WHAT'S IN A NAME?

KEY VERSE: ISAIAH 9:6

For a child will be born for us, a son will be given to us, and the government will be on His shoulders. He will be named Wonderful Counselor, Mighty God, Eternal Father, Prince of Peace.

Look closely at the names used to describe Jesus in this verse. Take a minute to think about them. Each title is one of honor and brings glory to Jesus. God sent Jesus as more than a Savior; He is described as mighty, wonderful, and eternal. He is the Prince of Peace. The amazing thing is He came to earth for you. Jesus wants to be a part of your life.

FAMILY TALK TIME

ASK YOUR KID:

What are some words your friends would use to describe you?

ASK YOUR PARENT:

What are some different titles you've had, and which has been your favorite?

BATTERIES NOT INCLUDED

KEY VERSE: 1 JOHN 2:2

He Himself is the propitiation for our sins, and not only for ours, but also for those of the whole world.

My son opened a birthday gift and quickly realized that the batteries hadn't been included! I checked our drawer, and we didn't have any! It was frustrating that my son couldn't play with his new toy. Jesus came to earth to be a sacrifice for all people. Jesus came to earth to save all God's chosen people. Everybody who chooses God is included in the salvation that He gives. Choose God and be included in His gift of forgiveness.

FAMILY TALK TIME

ASK YOUR KID:

What gift have you received that didn't include everything you needed?

ASK YOUR PARENT:

How would someone feel if he thought Jesus didn't come for his sins?

53

SEE IT OR BELIEVE IT

KEY VERSE: JOHN 4:42

And they told the woman, "We no longer believe because of what you said, for we have heard for ourselves and know that this really is the Savior of the world."

The Hubble telescope has seen objects in space as far as ten to fifteen billion light years away. Do you believe that fact, or do you need to see it for yourself? Sometimes seeing something makes it easier to believe rather than just hearing information. In today's key verse, people are able to recognize Jesus is the Savior based on what they have heard.

FAMILY TALK TIME

ASK YOUR KID:

Are you good with trusting what someone says, or do you have to see it to believe it?

ASK YOUR PARENT:

How are you able to believe in Jesus when you haven't seen Him?

54

BIG WORDS, BIGGER MEANING

KEY VERSE: MICAH 5:2

Bethlehem Ephrathah, you are small among the clans of Judah; One will come from you to be ruler over Israel for Me. His origin is from antiquity, from eternity.

Don't let some strange sounding words confuse you about the meaning of this verse. Ephrathah is a place, *origin* means beginning, *antiquity* means long ago, and *eternal* means forever. Once you figure out those words, this verse has a huge impact. From a small town called Bethlehem, the ruler over everything will appear. This ruler has existed in the past and will continue to exist forever and ever. Can you guess who I'm talking about? Jesus! Hundreds of years before His birth on earth, He was talked about.

FAMILY TALK TIME

ASK YOUR KID:

What do you usually do when you run across words you don't know or can't say when you're reading?

ASK YOUR PARENT:

Why is it important to stop and learn what words mean if you don't know them when you first see them?

55

SHEEP SAYS, "BAAA"

KEY VERSE: MATTHEW 2:6

You, Bethlehem, in the land of Judah, are by no means least among the leaders of Judah: because out of you will come a leader who will shepherd My people Israel.

Animal sounds are fun to teach younger children. You can call out an animal, and usually a toddler will respond with whatever sound that animal makes. For example, ask a small child, "What does a sheep say?" She will probably respond, "Baa!" In today's key verse, you discover another name for the Savior God promised was coming. God called Jesus a shepherd. Guess who the sheep are? Those who want to follow Jesus. Jesus was sent to earth to take care of those who believe in Him. Jesus served as a shepherd to those who followed Him. This isn't just long ago; Jesus is still a shepherd today.

FAMILY TALK TIME

ASK YOUR KID:

What do you know about a shepherd's job?

ASK YOUR PARENT:

What were my favorite animal sounds
to make when I was younger?

56

PAUL ADMITS TO GUILT

KEY VERSE: 1 TIMOTHY 1:15

This saying is trustworthy and deserving of full acceptance: "Christ Jesus came into the world to save sinners"—and I am the worst of them.

The missionary Paul was writing about himself in this verse. In his past, he hated Christians, and then he became one. That might have been hard to believe for people who knew Paul. Paul was clear about why Jesus came to earth. Paul said he was the worst, but the truth is that everybody is. No one is better than anyone else when it comes to sin. The great news is Jesus knew all of this all along. In fact, it's the reason He came to earth in the first place. No matter how badly you think you sinned, Jesus still died for you.

FAMILY TALK TIME

ASK YOUR KID:

Do you think some sins are worse than others?

ASK YOUR PARENT:

Why do you think Paul thought he was the worst?

WANTED: THE UNHEALTHY

KEY VERSE: MARK 2:17

When Jesus heard this, He told them, "Those who are well don't need a doctor, but the sick do need one. I didn't come to call the righteous, but sinners."

Being sick stinks, doesn't it? You don't feel well, you don't sleep well, and you can't hang out with your friends. This verse talks about being sick, but it's not the same kind of sickness as a sore throat or fever. What Jesus wanted people to understand was that He came to earth to help people. The people who need help are the sinners. The people who are sick are people who know they need Jesus in their daily lives in order to live a life that pleases God. Aren't you glad God sent Jesus to earth to help save sinners who need His help?

FAMILY TALK TIME

ASK YOUR KID:

When is the last time you got really sick?

ASK YOUR PARENT:

How is being physically sick and needing a doctor different from needing Jesus?

THE CHOICE

KEY VERSE: MATTHEW 12:18

"Here is My Servant whom I have chosen, My beloved in whom My soul delights; I will put My Spirit on Him, and He will proclaim justice to the nations."

God is talking about Jesus, His Son, in this verse. He has wonderful things to say about Him. Jesus is God's beloved and delights His soul. God makes it clear that He chose to allow Jesus to come to earth. You know how the story ends; Jesus died. God made the difficult choice to allow His Son, whom He loved dearly, to come to earth to die. Because God knows everything, He already knew what Jesus' death would be like. Yet God still chose to send Jesus to tell everyone about the possibility of eternal life with Him.

FAMILY TALK TIME

ASK YOUR KID:

What is one thing you don't think you could live without?

ASK YOUR PARENT:

What's the biggest sacrifice you've ever had to make?

59

WHO CAME FIRST?

KEY VERSE: JOHN 8:58

*Jesus said to them, "I assure you:
Before Abraham was, I am."*

The story of Abraham's life is told in the Old Testament.
Jesus' birth occurred in New Testament times. Reread
John 8:58. Who does it say came first? Jesus explained
that before Abraham lived, Jesus was. How is that possible? Some things you read in the Bible may be difficult
for you to understand, and that's okay! In this verse, Jesus
explained He always has been and always will be. His
earthly life began approximately two thousand years after
Abraham walked the earth, but Jesus has always been and
will always be.

FAMILY TALK TIME

ASK YOUR KID:

Whom do you ask for help when you don't understand something you read in the Bible?

ASK YOUR PARENT:

What do you do when you read something in the Bible you don't understand?

60

WHAT'S NEXT?

KEY VERSE: JOHN 17:24

"Father, I desire those You have given Me to be with Me where I am. Then they will see My glory, which You have given Me because You loved Me before the world's foundation."

God created the world. Humans sinned. God sent Jesus to the world. Jesus came to earth as a baby and grew up. What came next? Jesus told God He wants eternal life for sinners. He wants you to be with Him for eternity. You don't have to take a test and hope you pass. You don't have to worry if Jesus will change His mind. He wants you, no matter your past, present, or future.

FAMILY TALK TIME

ASK YOUR KID:

How does it make you to feel to know Jesus wants you to be with Him forever?

ASK YOUR PARENT:

What do you think Jesus' glory looks like?

61

PROVING A PROPHECY

KEY VERSE: MARK 15:27-28

They crucified two criminals with Him, one on His right and one on His left. [So Scripture was fulfilled that says: And He was counted among outlaws.]

What does it mean for Scripture to be fulfilled? Check out Isaiah 53:12. Many years before Jesus was born or crucified, Isaiah 53:12 included important facts about how Jesus would die. This prediction is called a prophecy, and it was proven true! Jesus was crucified between two men who were guilty of crimes. Jesus was innocent.

FAMILY TALK TIME

ASK YOUR KID:

Why do you think Jesus was crucified?

ASK YOUR PARENT:

Why do you think Jesus was crucified between two criminals?

62

SAVE YOURSELF

KEY VERSE: MARK 15:29-30

Those who passed by were yelling insults at Him, shaking their heads, and saying, "Ha! The One who would demolish the sanctuary and build it in three days, save Yourself by coming down from the cross!"

After Jesus was placed on the cross, He didn't die immediately. People weren't kind to Him and teased Him while He was suffering. You know Jesus is all-powerful, and He could have removed Himself from the cross. Do you know why He didn't? You. You are the reason. You, along with everyone else on earth, kept Jesus on the cross. He knew the sacrifice He was making, and He was committed to it. Jesus chose to save you forever over proving those people wrong in that moment. Jesus made the choice to stay on the cross.

FAMILY TALK TIME

ASK YOUR KID:

How do you think Jesus felt hearing those people yelling at Him on the cross?

ASK YOUR PARENT:

Do you think there are times when it's better to be quiet rather than to talk?

63

TOTAL DARKNESS

KEY VERSE: MARK 15:33-34

When it was noon, darkness came over the whole land until three in the afternoon. And at three Jesus cried out with a loud voice, "Eloi, Eloi, lemá sabachtháni?" which is translated, "My God, My God, why have You forsaken Me?"

Outer space is completely dark from the earth's view. According to scientists, that's because there are few molecules to scatter light. Light gets absorbed, or swallowed up, by the darkness. When Jesus called out to God, the earth became completely black. Can you imagine what it was like for complete darkness to cover the entire earth in the middle of the day? Darkness covered the earth when Jesus was separated from God.

FAMILY TALK TIME

ASK YOUR KID:

How do small kids react when they get separated from their parents?

ASK YOUR PARENT:

How did you feel the first time you left me with someone else to take care of me?

64

FULL ACCESS

KEY VERSE: MARK 15:37-39

Jesus let out a loud cry and breathed His last. Then the curtain of the sanctuary was split in two from top to bottom. When the centurion, who was standing opposite Him, saw the way He breathed His last, he said, "This man really was God's Son!"

The curtain that split in two from top to bottom was used to separate a holy area that the high priest alone could enter from the space everyone could enter. A rope was actually tied to the priest's foot in case he died while he was in there so his body could be drug out! The tearing of the curtain made it clear that now everyone has access to God, not just the high priest in the sanctuary. Even a guard watching Jesus die recognized Jesus was God's Son. How incredible was it for this guard to see with his own eyes exactly who Jesus is!

FAMILY TALK TIME

ASK YOUR KID:

Why do you think God tore the curtain from the top to the bottom?

ASK YOUR PARENT:

What does having full access to God mean to you?

PILATE'S SURPRISE

KEY VERSE: MARK 15:44-45

Pilate was surprised that He was already dead. Summoning the centurion, he asked him whether He had already died. When he found out from the centurion, he gave the corpse to Joseph.

Why was Pilate surprised Jesus was already dead? Dying by crucifixion often took several days, but Jesus didn't even live for twenty-four hours on the cross. This didn't surprise Jesus, though. Jesus chose to die. At any moment, Jesus could have gotten off the cross, but He didn't. He made the choice to die because He knew it meant you would be able to live with Him forever if you make the choice to do so. While Pilate was surprised by Jesus' quick death, it was no accident or surprise to Jesus Himself.

FAMILY TALK TIME

ASK YOUR KID:

What can God do that would surprise you?

ASK YOUR PARENT:

How do you handle surprises?

66

DETAILS MATTER

KEY VERSE: MARK 15:46-47

After he bought some fine linen, he took Him down and wrapped Him in the linen. Then he placed Him in a tomb cut out of the rock, and rolled a stone against the entrance to the tomb. Now Mary Magdalene and Mary the mother of Jesus were watching where He was placed.

What kind of moon was in the sky last night? Was it full, a crescent shape, or a half-moon? While some people are great with remembering details like the shape of the moon, others aren't. The Bible makes it clear Jesus' body was put in a tomb and witnesses saw where He was placed. These details matter, and it's an important part of recognizing the power of Jesus in the days after His death. Including information from eyewitnesses makes it even more difficult for someone to say Jesus didn't conquer death.

FAMILY TALK TIME

ASK YOUR KID:

What kind of details are easiest for you to remember?

ASK YOUR PARENT:

Why are eyewitnesses important to an event?

67

WHAT'S GOING ON?

KEY VERSE: MARK 16:4-5

Looking up, they observed that the stone—which was very large—had been rolled away. When they entered the tomb, they saw a young man dressed in a long white robe sitting on the right side; they were amazed and alarmed.

Remember the women who saw the stone put in front of the tomb holding Jesus' body? They came back to prepare Jesus' body with spices and linens. When they arrived, they were surprised to see the stone had been rolled away. The women are described as "amazed and alarmed." The man they saw wasn't Jesus. Imagine what they were thinking. Where is Jesus? I know this is where His body was. The man in the robe didn't make the women wait long for an explanation.

FAMILY TALK TIME

ASK YOUR KID:

When is the last time you were surprised by what you saw?

ASK YOUR PARENT:

Why did the women at Jesus' tomb have mixed emotions?

68

NO ONE TO SEE HERE!

KEY VERSE: MARK 16:6

"Don't be alarmed," he told them. "You are looking for Jesus the Nazarene, who was crucified. He has been resurrected! He is not here! See the place where they put Him."

"Nothing to see here, folks! Move along!" Has anyone ever told you that? In today's key verse, no one was being rushed away from the empty tomb. Jesus came back from the dead. He died on the cross, stayed dead for three days, and then He rose again! The man in the robe delivered the news to the women who came to prepare Jesus' body. The place where Jesus' body had been placed was empty. There was nothing to see!

FAMILY TALK TIME

ASK YOUR KID:

How do you think the women felt when they learned Jesus was alive?

ASK YOUR PARENT:

Why is it good to see something for yourself, like the women seeing the empty tomb?

I TOLD YOU SO!

KEY VERSE: MARK 16:7

Go, tell His disciples and Peter, "He is going ahead of you to Galilee; you will see Him there just as He told you."

Has your mom ever made you wear a coat even when you thought it was too hot? Did the temperature drop quickly and make you so glad you had the coat? Your mom could say, "I told you so!" in that situation. In today's verse, the angel is very clear that Jesus already told everyone that He was coming back. Why were the women amazed at the news? Jesus did exactly what He promised He would do. He always has, and He always will keep His promises. What Jesus says He will do, He does.

FAMILY TALK TIME

ASK YOUR KID:

Why is it hard to do what we ask you to do sometimes, especially when it doesn't make sense to you?

ASK YOUR PARENT:

How is Jesus able to keep every single promise He's made?

70

SPEECHLESS

KEY VERSE: MARK 16:8

They went out and started running from the tomb, because trembling and astonishment overwhelmed them. And they said nothing to anyone, since they were afraid.

"I have so much to do. I don't know how I'll ever get it done!" This is a popular comment by people who feel overwhelmed. Being overwhelmed feels like you're buried underneath a pile of too much to do or think about. While Jesus had made it clear He wouldn't stay dead, the women who saw the empty tomb were overwhelmed. They were filled with so many emotions that they found themselves unable to speak. The women had the best news to share, and instead they were speechless.

FAMILY TALK TIME

ASK YOUR KID:

Have you ever found yourself
speechless, and if so, why?

ASK YOUR PARENT:

What makes people feel overwhelmed?

71

CONFESSION IS NEEDED

KEY VERSE: 1 JOHN 1:9

If we confess our sins, He is faithful and righteous to forgive us our sins and to cleanse us from all unrighteousness.

Once I broke a really nice dish that had been a wedding present for my friend's mom. Instead of telling her, my friend and I hid the broken dish. I felt terrible about it, my friend's mom found the broken plate, and I got in trouble anyway! Guilt can drive you crazy. When you know you've done wrong, the best thing to do is confess, or tell, God about it. When you are honest with God, the sacrifice Jesus made on the cross covers your guilt.

FAMILY TALK TIME

ASK YOUR KID:

What have you done wrong that you had a hard time admitting to?

ASK YOUR PARENT:

Why is it better to admit your wrongdoing right away instead of waiting?

72

SAVED BY GRACE

KEY VERSE: EPHESIANS 2:4-5

God, who is rich in mercy, because of His great love that He had for us, made us alive with the Messiah even though we were dead in trespasses. You are saved by grace!

Grace is receiving something you don't deserve. Mercy is choosing to show kindness toward someone who isn't deserving of it. Jesus offers you both grace and mercy. Thank goodness Jesus doesn't give you what you deserve! Jesus knows all about you, and He chooses to forgive you. Jesus sets the ultimate example of how to treat others through the way He treats all people. Think about how you treated the last person who was unkind to you. Remember Jesus' example and follow it.

FAMILY TALK TIME

ASK YOUR KID:

What's something you've received
that you didn't deserve?

ASK YOUR PARENT:

Which is easier to give to others:
grace or mercy?

FAITH, NOT WORKS

KEY VERSE: EPHESIANS 2:8-9

*You are saved by grace through faith,
and this is not from yourselves; it is God's
gift—not from works, so that no one can boast.*

Have your parents ever told you that you have to do jobs around the house to earn your allowance? When you complete certain jobs like cleaning the bathroom or vacuuming, you get paid a small amount of money. The more you work, the more money you can earn. That's not how you get into heaven, though. You can't work your way to heaven. Jesus doesn't give you a list of things to do and give you a ticket into heaven once you check them off. Faith in Jesus Christ enables you to admit you are a sinner, believe in Jesus as your Savior and Lord, and confess Jesus as Lord over your life. Have you accepted God's free gift of salvation?

FAMILY TALK TIME

ASK YOUR KID:

What's your favorite job to do
around the house?

ASK YOUR PARENT:

Why is it hard for some people to understand
that God's gift of salvation is free?

CREATED FOR GOOD

KEY VERSE: EPHESIANS 2:10

We are His creation, created in Christ Jesus for good works, which God prepared ahead of time so that we should walk in them.

Do you like to paint? Maybe you are a great cook, or perhaps you're an expert with building blocks. How does it feel when you paint a beautiful painting, cook a great dish, or complete a complicated structure? Working hard makes you feel good, doesn't it? God created you to do good works for Him. Jesus sacrificed His earthly life so that you could have eternal life with Him. God's plans include you helping Him spread the word about God's amazing gift of salvation.

FAMILY TALK TIME

ASK YOUR KID:

What is a project you've worked hard on that you felt good about finishing?

ASK YOUR PARENT:

How does knowing God created you to do good affect how you live?

75

A GIFT OF LOVE

KEY VERSE: EPHESIANS 5:2

Walk in love, as the Messiah also loved us and gave Himself for us, a sacrificial and fragrant offering to God.

One night when I was a little girl, I told my mom, "You can't make me!" as we were leaving church. Not only was it disrespectful, another kid heard me and used the same line on his parents. Boy, did I get in trouble! No one made Jesus sacrifice Himself on the cross. Jesus died for you because He loves you. Just like you have a choice to follow Jesus, Jesus had a choice to offer you eternal life. Jesus gave His life as a sacrifice for you. When you really think about what Jesus did for you, you realize how important it is to share Jesus' incredible love with anyone who will listen.

FAMILY TALK TIME

ASK YOUR KID:

What's your favorite kind of gift to receive?

ASK YOUR PARENT:

What makes someone a good gift-giver?

76

NOTHING ELSE MATTERS

KEY VERSE: PHILIPPIANS 3:8

More than that, I also consider everything to be a loss in view of the surpassing value of knowing Christ Jesus my Lord. Because of Him I have suffered the loss of all things and consider them filth, so that I may gain Christ.

Do you put your shoes in the same place when you come home every day? Putting them in the same place will help you not lose them. This way they'll be ready when you need to put them on the next time you go out. In most cases, losing something, like one shoe out of a pair, is frustrating! In today's verse, losing is a good thing. How valuable is knowing God as your personal Lord and Savior? According to this verse, nothing else matters when you have Christ as your Savior. Gaining Christ is worth the loss of everything else.

FAMILY TALK TIME

ASK YOUR KID:

What do you do when you've lost something important to you?

ASK YOUR PARENT:

How much value does Philippians 3:8 put on knowing Christ?

77

THAT'S STRONG LOVE!

KEY VERSE: ROMANS 8:38-39

I am persuaded that not even death or life, angels or rulers, things present or things to come, hostile powers, height or depth, or any other created thing will have the power to separate us from the love of God that is in Christ Jesus our Lord!

What is your favorite restaurant? How far are you willing to go to get there? How long would you wait for a table? How much would you pay for your favorite dish? When you love something, you're willing to make sacrifices. Jesus made a great sacrifice out of His love for us.

Take a look at all the things that can't separate you from God's love in today's key verses. Nothing has the power to separate you from God! You are never without Jesus' love. You can't go too far way, you can't sin too many times, and you can't make Jesus change His mind about you.

FAMILY TALK TIME

ASK YOUR KID:

What's something you love to do with your family?

ASK YOUR PARENT:

How would you explain Jesus' love for people to someone who has never heard of Jesus before?

78

A CRAZY KIND OF LOVE

KEY VERSE: EPHESIANS 3:19

*Know the Messiah's love that surpasses knowledge,
so you may be filled with all the fullness of God.*

What do you do when you have trouble understanding something? Maybe it's something new you're learning in school, the way a friend treated you, or something that is happening in your life that makes no sense. While you may be able to find the answer to what's troubling you eventually, there's one thing you will never be able to fully understand—God's love for you. The Bible is clear; God loves you beyond anything you will ever understand here on earth. That crazy kind of love is why God sent Jesus to earth, so you have the opportunity to receive the gift of salvation that He offers. Once you have the love God offers, don't you want others to know about it too?

FAMILY TALK TIME

ASK YOUR KID:

What do you do when you have trouble understanding something? How do you deal with it?

ASK YOUR PARENT:

What's the benefit of realizing you can't ever really understand God's love for you?

79

NO TELESCOPE NEEDED

KEY VERSE: COLOSSIANS 2:9-10

The entire fullness of God's nature dwells bodily in Christ, and you have been filled by Him, who is the head over every ruler and authority.

Telescopes are amazing creations. They allow you to see things far out in space, to study stars, and to sometimes even catch a glimpse of another planet! You don't have to use a telescope to see how powerful Christ is. Without Christ, the universe would be nothing. How amazing to know that the One in charge of it all rules over all things on heaven and earth. Jesus completes you!

FAMILY TALK TIME

ASK YOUR KID:

What can you name that Jesus is not over or in control of?

ASK YOUR PARENT:

Why is it important to remember Jesus completes you?

80

LIVING BY FAITH

KEY VERSE: GALATIANS 2:19-20

Through the law I have died to the law, so that I might live for God. I have been crucified with Christ and I no longer live, but Christ lives in me. The life I now live in the body, I live by faith in the Son of God, who loved me and gave Himself for me.

When you accept God's gift of salvation, you are inviting Christ into your life forever. Once you've made the decision to follow Christ, He will never leave you, and your life will be changed forever for the better. Living by faith requires you to allow God to lead you in the way you talk, how you treat others, and the decisions you make. Becoming a Christian is possible because of Jesus' sacrifice. When you live for Christ, you honor Jesus for all He has done for you. Jesus matters more than anything else in your life.

FAMILY TALK TIME

ASK YOUR KID:

What are some ways you can live for Christ?

ASK YOUR PARENT:

How do others know you are living for Christ?

81

CAN I GET A WITNESS?

KEY VERSE: ACTS 1:8

"You will receive power when the Holy Spirit has come upon you, and you will be My witnesses in Jerusalem, in all Judea and Samaria, and to the ends of the earth."

Have you ever been a witness of something? Of course you have! A witness is someone who sees an event happen and can tell others about it. Jesus wants you to be a witness for Him. Do you have to go to Jerusalem, Judea, and Samaria? You can, but you don't have to travel that far! You can tell others about Jesus' love wherever you go. Who do you know who needs to hear about Jesus today?

FAMILY TALK TIME

ASK YOUR KID:

Where can you go and be a witness for Jesus?

ASK YOUR PARENT:

What are some important things to tell others about Jesus?

FIGHT FORGETFULNESS

KEY VERSE: JOHN 14:26

"The Counselor, the Holy Spirit—the Father will send Him in My name—will teach you all things and remind you of everything I have told you."

Do you ever walk in a room and forget why you went in there in the first place? The Bible is full of information to study, learn, and live out. No matter how many times you read the Bible, you will never run out of things to learn. How is it possible for you to remember everything you read? The good news is you don't have to worry about forgetting what the Bible says. God promises to remind you of everything He wants you to know. When you need help remembering something, you can always ask God for help!

FAMILY TALK TIME

ASK YOUR KID:

What's the last thing you had
to be reminded to do?

ASK YOUR PARENT:

When is it okay to ask God to help you
remember something?

SOME EXCLUSIONS APPLY

KEY VERSE: MARK 16:15

[Jesus] said to them, "Go into all the world and preach the gospel to the whole creation."

At the end of a commercial advertising a great sale, have you ever heard the saying, "Some exclusions apply"? This usually means certain brands or items aren't on sale, or there's a limit on the number of items you can buy. The word exclusion means something is left out. God's command to tell others about Jesus applies to everyone. God wants all people to know about the good news of Jesus Christ. Remember when you meet people that no one is excluded from hearing about Jesus' ultimate sacrifice.

FAMILY TALK TIME

ASK YOUR KID:

Where do you have to go to tell others about Jesus?

ASK YOUR PARENT:

What's the longest distance you've ever traveled, and where did you go?

84

SATISFACTION GUARANTEED

KEY VERSE: HEBREWS 13:5

Your life should be free from the love of money.
Be satisfied with what you have, for He Himself
has said, I will never leave you or forsake you.

"Satisfaction is guaranteed, or your money back!" What do you have to lose when someone promises you can return something if you aren't happy with it? Being satisfied means having all you need. God promises never to leave you, and you can have peace knowing God provides you with everything you need.

FAMILY TALK TIME

ASK YOUR KID:

Why does God want you to be happy with what you have?

ASK YOUR PARENT:

What's the last thing you returned to the store because you weren't satisfied with it?

85

CASTING YOUR CARES ON GOD

KEY VERSE: 1 PETER 5:7

Casting all your care on Him, because He cares about you.

Fly-fishing involves casting your rod back and forth in the water in hopes of catching a fish. *Casting* means to throw something really hard in a specific direction. God already knows you will face hard times and choices. God wants you to give your struggles to Him. He already knows what you are dealing with before you tell Him, whether it is bullying, divorce, anger, or sadness. Give your troubles to God. Not only can He handle anything you give Him, He *wants* to help you. God created you and cares for you more than you'll ever be able to understand.

FAMILY TALK TIME

ASK YOUR KID:

What's something you've been worrying about that you need to give to God?

ASK YOUR PARENT:

How does remembering God cares for you help you during tough times?

86

THE GUARDER OF YOUR HEART

KEY VERSE: PHILIPPIANS 4:6-7

Don't worry about anything, but in everything, through prayer and petition with thanksgiving, let your requests be made known to God. And the peace of God, which surpasses every thought, will guard your hearts and minds in Christ Jesus.

Guards are posted in specific places to protect people, monuments, special equipment, and many other things. When you see a guard, you know something or someone important is nearby. When you need God's help, He is there for you. When you are worried about something happening in your life, you can tell God about it. That's exactly what God wants you to do! God promises a peace that comes from Jesus only will protect you. Jesus is the guard of your heart.

FAMILY TALK TIME

ASK YOUR KID:

Where have you seen guards before,
and why were they there?

ASK YOUR PARENT:

Why does God want you to pray when He
already knows what you'll say?

MAKE GOOD CHOICES

KEY VERSE: 2 TIMOTHY 1:7

*God has not given us a spirit of fearfulness,
but one of power, love, and sound judgment.*

If God promises to forgive you of your sins, is it okay to sin as much as you want? While God knows you will make mistakes, He wants you to do your best to make good choices. God doesn't want you walking around making mistakes and getting in trouble. God wants you to do your best to make choices that are pleasing to Him, and that's what is meant by the words *sound judgment* in today's key verse. Do your best and leave the rest up to God.

FAMILY TALK TIME

ASK YOUR KID:

Why doesn't God want you to be afraid?

ASK YOUR PARENT:

When have you recently made a choice that you know was pleasing to God?

PICKING THE PROPER TIME

KEY VERSE: HEBREWS 4:16

Let us approach the throne of grace with boldness, so that we may receive mercy and find grace to help us at the proper time.

Meteor showers occur several times during the year. But if you walk out in your backyard any random night and expect to see a meteor shower, you'll likely be disappointed. You have to know the proper time to look and have good sky conditions to see a meteor shower in all its glory. While God knows you sin, He still wants to hear from you. When you are honest with God about the decisions you've made that weren't good, He promises to offer forgiveness instead of punishment. God promises to forgive and offer you exactly what you need, when you need it!

FAMILY TALK TIME

ASK YOUR KID:

When is the best time to talk to God?

ASK YOUR PARENT:

How does God know what you need
and when you need it?

89

SEARCHING FOR STRENGTH

KEY VERSE: PSALM 73:25-26

Who do I have in heaven but You? And I desire nothing on earth but You. My flesh and my heart may fail, but God is the strength of my heart, my portion forever.

When someone desires something, it means he or she really wants it. Maybe you desire to walk on the moon one day, or you desire a break from school. Even when you do things that disappoint God, He still desires you. When your body is weak and tired, God is there. You don't have to rely on physical strength to survive. God promises ultimate strength that never dies or gets tired. Ask God to help you keep your focus on Him so that you only want and need Him.

FAMILY TALK TIME

ASK YOUR KID:

What's the heaviest thing you've ever picked up?

ASK YOUR PARENT:

When have you asked God to give you the strength to do something?

90

MISSION POSSIBLE

KEY VERSE: 1 CORINTHIANS 10:13

No temptation has overtaken you except what is common to humanity. God is faithful, and He will not allow you to be tempted beyond what you are able, but with the temptation He will also provide a way of escape so that you are able to bear it.

A popular game locks people in a room for one hour while they use clues to try to figure their way out. At the end of the hour, you either celebrate being able to get out or the door is unlocked for you. You either have officially escaped, or you give up. God knows you'll be tempted by sin. You have choices to make, but the great news is you don't have to wonder if you'll be able to escape temptation. God promises you will always have a way out of sin, but it's your decision whether or not you take it.

FAMILY TALK TIME

ASK YOUR KID:

What are some temptations for you and your friends today?

ASK YOUR PARENT:

What is one way God has allowed you the chance to escape temptation?

SEEK GOD

KEY VERSE: ZEPHANIAH 2:3

Seek the Lord, all you humble of the earth, who carry out what He commands. Seek righteousness, seek humility.

When you play hide-and-seek with friends, do you enjoy doing the hiding or being the seeker? When you are the seeker, your goal is to find those hiding, right? When you are seeking something, you are trying to find it. Zephaniah 2:3 tells you to seek three things: the Lord, righteousness, and humility. This means God wants you to look for Him, for ways to be and do good, and for the ability to put others before yourself. When you focus on these three things, it pleases God. God's not hiding; He's always there for you.

FAMILY TALK TIME

ASK YOUR KID:

What's the longest it has taken for someone to find you when playing hide-and-seek?

ASK YOUR PARENT:

Why is it hard for some people to be humble?

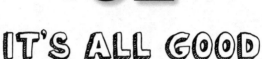

IT'S ALL GOOD

KEY VERSE: ROMANS 8:28

We know that all things work together for the good of those who love God: those who are called according to His purpose.

You got a bad grade on a test, your sister hurt your feelings, a friend can't spend the night, and your game just got canceled because of thunder. None of those things sound like fun, do they? The truth is you will have times that things don't go your way. Some things you may have control over, and other things you don't. The amazing thing is God does have control over everything. Anything that happens in your life—good or bad—can be used by God. God can use even your mistakes! Sin does mess things up, but God has the power to make things good.

FAMILY TALK TIME

ASK YOUR KID:

How do you think God is able to make something good out of something bad?

ASK YOUR PARENT:

What is a bad thing that's happened to you that God used for good?

93

FELLOWSHIP CAFÉ

KEY VERSE: 1 CORINTHIANS 1:9

God is faithful; you were called by Him into fellowship with His Son, Jesus Christ our Lord.

On Wednesday nights, my church has Fellowship Café. Dinner is cooked, and we crowd around tables to enjoy fellowship together. We talk about our week so far, laugh, encourage each other, and of course, we eat dinner! Fellowship is fun! Jesus' death on the cross provides the possibility of fellowship with Him. This means Jesus wants to enjoy a relationship with you. God's promise to be faithful means once you've made the decision to become a Christian, you've gained fellowship with Jesus. You can communicate with Jesus anytime, anywhere, about anything.

FAMILY TALK TIME

ASK YOUR KID:

How do you think fellowship with Jesus should be?

ASK YOUR PARENT:

Why is it important to fellowship with Christians and with Jesus?

94

WITHOUT WAVERING

KEY VERSE: HEBREWS 10:23

Let us hold on to the confession of our hope without wavering, for He who promised is faithful.

On a popular reality TV show, contestants are put through physical challenges to win rewards. One challenge involves balancing on a small area for as long as possible in the hot sun. After a few minutes, the contestants start to waver back and forth before eventually falling off. Once you place your hope in God, you don't ever have to waver or worry about being let down by God. Putting your faith in God is the best decision you can make!

FAMILY TALK TIME

ASK YOUR KID:

What's the longest you are able to balance on one foot?

ASK YOUR PARENT:

How does knowing that God never breaks His promises give you hope?

95

A FRESH START

KEY VERSE: LAMENTATIONS 3:22-23

Because of the LORD's faithful love we do not perish, for His mercies never end. They are new every morning; great is Your faithfulness!

When one bad thing happens, does it ruin your whole day? As hard as you may try not to, as a human, you are going to sin each day. God already knows this. This verse is a great reminder that God has compassion for you. He cares about what happens in your life. Every morning is a new chance to begin again. Praise God for His faithfulness to never give up on you! Ask God for a fresh start, and watch how God's love for you changes the way you handle what comes your way.

FAMILY TALK TIME

ASK YOUR KID:

Would you consider yourself a morning person, an afternoon person, or a night person?

ASK YOUR PARENT:

How does God's compassion compare to the compassion people show to one another?

96

WRONG PLUS RIGHT

KEY VERSE: ROMANS 3:3-4

What then? If some did not believe, will their unbelief cancel God's faithfulness? Absolutely not! God must be true, even if everyone is a liar, as it is written: That You may be justified in Your words and triumph when You judge.

Two wrongs don't make a right, do they? If people don't have faith in God, does that mean God's faithfulness doesn't exist? According to today's key verses, the answer is an absolute no! Even when people choose not to believe in God, He's still there. Even when people choose not to put their faith in God, God still promises to be faithful to those who follow Him. You don't have to worry about if God will be faithful to keep His promises. God's actions are not based on the way people treat Him. Aren't you glad?

FAMILY TALK TIME

ASK YOUR KID:

Why do you think some people choose not to believe in God?

ASK YOUR PARENT:

How hard is it to be kind to people who aren't kind to you?

LITTLE THINGS MATTER

KEY VERSE: LUKE 16:10

"Whoever is faithful in very little is also faithful in much, and whoever is unrighteous in very little is also unrighteous in much."

One day I was running very early in the morning. It was still dark out, and I was enjoying the beautiful sky filled with stars. I looked up and saw a woman who was following the rules of the neighborhood in the way she was taking care of her dog. Did she know I was going to be there? No. In fact, I scared her a little bit! She chose to follow the rules even when she thought no one was looking. God rewards those who follow Him in whatever they do. No decision is too small for God to honor. Putting your faith in God in everything you do brings blessings.

FAMILY TALK TIME

ASK YOUR KID:

What's something you've done lately that pleases God, but no one knows about it?

ASK YOUR PARENT:

Why is it important to stay faithful to God in everything you do?

98

WATCH OUT!

KEY VERSE: COLOSSIANS 2:8

Be careful that no one takes you captive through philosophy and empty deceit based on human tradition, based on the elemental forces of the world, and not based on Christ.

When God created man, He knew some people wouldn't believe in Him. Since God created the world and everything in it, living your life as a Christian is based on Jesus' teaching and example. Not everyone believes in Jesus' teachings. Some of those unbelievers will try to trick you and confuse you about what you believe about God. This verse is a warning to watch out for those who might try to trick you. You won't ever know everything there is to know about Jesus, and that's okay. Remember to read your Bible and trust what God has written in the Scriptures.

FAMILY TALK TIME

ASK YOUR KID:

When has someone tried to play a trick on you? Did it work?

ASK YOUR PARENT:

How should you treat people who don't believe in Jesus?

99

CHOOSING SIDES

KEY VERSE: ROMANS 8:31

If God is for us, who is against us?

God controls everything. He made the earth, He made man, and He sent Jesus to be the Savior of the world. When you make the important decision to follow Christ by becoming a Christian, you are choosing to side with Christ. When God is on your side, does it really matter who is on the other side? You will face lots of choices in the future. Some will be easy to make, and others will take thought and prayer. The next time you need help, remember the God of the universe is on your side.

FAMILY TALK TIME

ASK YOUR KID:

How does it make you feel to know
God is on your side?

ASK YOUR PARENT:

Why does it not matter who is against you
when God is on your side?

100

SET YOUR MIND

KEY VERSE: 2 TIMOTHY 1:9

He has saved us and called us with a holy calling, not according to our works, but according to His own purpose and grace, which was given to us in Christ Jesus before time began.

Before God created the universe, the plan was in place. You didn't do anything to earn eternal life; Jesus chose to sacrifice Himself for you. You do make the choice whether or not to receive the gift Jesus offers. Once you accept God's grace and mercy, you have a holy calling! What you say and do matters because you represent Jesus to others. It's time to spread the great news of Jesus to those who need to hear about Him.

FAMILY TALK TIME

ASK YOUR KID:

Who do you know who needs to hear
the good news of Jesus?

ASK YOUR PARENT:

What do you think about having a holy calling?